MAYER SMITH

Eclipsed by Your Light

Copyright © 2025 by Mayer Smith

All rights reserved. No part of this publication may be reproduced, stored or transmitted in any form or by any means, electronic, mechanical, photocopying, recording, scanning, or otherwise without written permission from the publisher. It is illegal to copy this book, post it to a website, or distribute it by any other means without permission.

This novel is entirely a work of fiction. The names, characters and incidents portrayed in it are the work of the author's imagination. Any resemblance to actual persons, living or dead, events or localities is entirely coincidental.

Mayer Smith asserts the moral right to be identified as the author of this work.

Mayer Smith has no responsibility for the persistence or accuracy of URLs for external or third-party Internet Websites referred to in this publication and does not guarantee that any content on such Websites is, or will remain, accurate or appropriate.

Designations used by companies to distinguish their products are often claimed as trademarks. All brand names and product names used in this book and on its cover are trade names, service marks, trademarks and registered trademarks of their respective owners. The publishers and the book are not associated with any product or vendor mentioned in this book. None of the companies referenced within the book have endorsed the book.

First edition

*This book was professionally typeset on Reedsy.
Find out more at reedsy.com*

Contents

1	The Unseen Connection	1
2	A Light in the Darkness	7
3	Shattered Illusions	14
4	The Mask Beneath	20
5	Into the Abyss	27
6	The Whispering Shadows	34
7	Secrets in the Bloodline	40
8	Unraveling Threads	47
9	The Heart of Darkness	54
10	The Final Veil	61
11	Embraced by Light	68
12	Embraced by the Shadows	74

One

The Unseen Connection

Lara Whitaker stood at the grand ballroom entrance, the heavy velvet curtains casting deep shadows over the polished marble floor. The sound of laughter and clinking glasses echoed in the distance, but she was still, almost as if the noise couldn't reach her. It was the kind of night where everything seemed poised on the edge of something—a moment suspended in time, waiting to tip into either brilliance or chaos.

The gala was an annual affair, a display of opulence and status for the city's elite. Lara had attended more of these events than she cared to count, always the observer, always the one on the outside looking in. But tonight, something felt different. Maybe it was the weight of expectation pressing down on her shoulders, or perhaps it was the slight tremor in her chest that hadn't been there before. Either way, she couldn't shake the feeling that tonight would change everything.

She smoothed the fabric of her dress—midnight blue, the kind that shimmered under the chandelier light like a piece of the night sky—and adjusted the sleek strands of her hair that framed her face. She wasn't one for being noticed, and yet, tonight, she couldn't help but feel as if someone was waiting for her to make her entrance.

"Lara, darling! You made it!"

She turned to find her best friend, Amelia, making her way through the crowd, her heels clicking sharply on the marble floor. Amelia was always the life of the party, her laughter carrying through the room like music. She wore a dress of fire-engine red, a contrast to Lara's quieter, more somber blue.

Amelia's eyes sparkled with mischief as she pulled Lara into a tight hug. "You look stunning. Just perfect for tonight. I can already feel the excitement in the air."

Lara chuckled softly, though it didn't quite reach her eyes. "You always say that."

"That's because it's true. But seriously," Amelia said, her voice dropping to a conspiratorial whisper, "there's someone here tonight who's been dying to meet you. He's been asking about you since the moment he walked in."

Lara raised an eyebrow. "Who?"

Amelia didn't answer right away. She simply gave Lara a knowing smile before gesturing toward a cluster of well-

The Unseen Connection

dressed guests gathered near the bar. At the center of the group was a man—tall, with dark, almost impossibly perfect features. His hair was tousled in a way that looked deliberate, and his expression was unreadable, like a man who'd seen too much of the world but was still too detached to be touched by it.

He was studying the crowd, his sharp gaze sweeping over the room as if searching for something—or someone. And then, as if feeling Lara's stare, his eyes locked onto hers.

For a moment, time seemed to stand still. The people around them blurred, and the sounds of the gala faded into the background. His gaze was intense, piercing, as though he saw right through her, beyond the polished surface and into the dark corners of her mind. Lara felt her pulse quicken, her breath catching in her throat.

"Who is he?" Lara asked, her voice quieter than she intended.

Amelia smirked, clearly enjoying Lara's reaction. "That's Elijah Grayson. He's an artist, though most people around here don't care much for that. He's… a bit of an enigma. No one really knows much about him."

Lara's curiosity piqued, though she couldn't help but feel a little unnerved. There was something about him that seemed too intense, too…otherworldly.

"He's looking at me," Lara whispered, her eyes still locked with his.

Eclipsed by Your Light

Amelia laughed, clearly unbothered by the attention. "Of course he is. He's been asking about you, Lara. You've been on his mind since he saw your name on the guest list."

The words hit Lara like a rush of cold air. She wasn't used to being the center of attention, especially not from someone like Elijah Grayson. She knew nothing about him, yet the way he looked at her—eyes dark and full of something she couldn't quite name—felt like a storm waiting to break.

She forced herself to look away, taking a small step back, though she could feel his presence pulling at her like gravity. The air around her seemed charged, as though the space between them had become too small to ignore.

"What's he like?" Lara asked, her voice betraying the curiosity she was trying so hard to suppress.

Amelia shrugged. "He's aloof. Mysterious. People think he's got a dark side, but no one really knows. He keeps to himself mostly, and when he does speak, it's… well, you'll see."

Before Lara could respond, the crowd around them shifted, and Elijah made his way toward her, his movements slow but purposeful. His gaze never wavered as he approached, the air around him thick with unspoken tension.

Lara's heart raced, an odd mixture of anticipation and something else—something she couldn't quite identify. He stopped just a few feet away, and for a long, heavy moment, neither of them said anything. His presence was like a magnet, pulling her in despite the fact that every instinct told her to step back.

"Miss Whitaker," he said, his voice low, almost a murmur, but it cut through the noise of the room like a blade. His accent was rich, smooth, with a trace of something foreign—something that made the hairs on the back of her neck stand up. "It's a pleasure to finally meet you."

Lara's breath caught. She hadn't expected the sound of his voice to be so… entrancing. "I… I didn't know we'd met before."

"We haven't," he replied, his lips curling into a slight, knowing smile. "But I feel as though I've known you longer than I should."

The words hung in the air, weighted with something that felt dangerously close to fate. It was absurd. She didn't know this man. She couldn't know him.

Yet somehow, she felt like she did.

Lara opened her mouth to speak, but nothing came out. Elijah didn't seem to mind. His eyes flicked over her, slow and deliberate, as though memorizing every detail. "You've been on my mind since I heard about your work," he said softly, the words almost drowned by the music swirling around them. "But it's more than that. There's something… familiar about you."

Her chest tightened, the strange sense of déjà vu settling over her like a heavy fog. She could feel the weight of his gaze on her skin, the intensity of it seeping into her bones.

"Perhaps it's your art," she said, her voice barely above a whisper, trying to ground herself in something, anything. "I've heard your work is... evocative."

"Elusive," he corrected, his smile widening ever so slightly. "Yes, I suppose that's a better word for it."

The silence between them deepened. Around them, the party continued, but Lara felt as though they were in a bubble, a separate world entirely. She couldn't explain it, but her pulse was thundering in her ears, her thoughts scattered like leaves in the wind. There was something about this man—this Elijah—that drew her in, something dangerous and magnetic, as if he were a shadow and she was the light that would either expose him or consume him.

He stepped closer, his eyes never leaving hers. "May I have this dance?" he asked, his voice almost a challenge.

Lara hesitated, heart pounding against her ribs. She didn't dance. She never danced. But something in his eyes... something about him made her forget every rule she'd ever made.

"Yes," she heard herself say, her voice barely above a breath.

As Elijah led her into the center of the room, the world around them seemed to fade away, leaving only the two of them in the center of the storm.

Two

A Light in the Darkness

The night air was cool against Lara's skin as she stepped out of the grand ballroom, her pulse still racing from the encounter with Elijah. The heavy doors closed behind her with a soft thud, cutting off the hum of voices and music, leaving her in the eerie silence of the garden courtyard. She needed air. She needed to think.

Her heart was still beating erratically, each thrum echoing through her chest. The touch of Elijah's hand on her waist as he guided her in the dance lingered like an electric current, a spark she couldn't shake. He had been close—too close. The scent of his cologne, dark and woody, mixed with the faint trace of cigar smoke, had woven itself into her senses, leaving her feeling both unnerved and… strangely drawn to him.

She walked aimlessly, her heels clicking softly against the stone path, the sound swallowed by the thick shadows that draped the garden. The air had a crisp bite to it, the kind that made her inhale deeply, trying to clear her mind. The moon hung low in the sky, casting a pale silver glow over the manicured hedges and blooming roses. The stillness of the night, punctuated only by the distant call of an owl, felt like a contrast to the storm that raged inside her.

"Lara?"

The voice came from behind her, smooth and unexpectedly close. She froze, her breath hitching in her throat as her body tensed. She hadn't heard him approach. Hadn't sensed him at all. And yet there he was, standing just a few feet away, his silhouette outlined by the soft moonlight. Elijah.

"I didn't mean to startle you," he said, his tone low, almost apologetic, though there was no trace of hesitation in his presence. He was there, like a shadow, looming with the quiet confidence of a man who was accustomed to being noticed.

Lara swallowed hard, turning slowly to face him. "You didn't startle me," she replied, though her voice came out a little breathier than she intended. Her pulse quickened again, the rapid thumping in her chest a reminder of just how disarmed he had left her earlier.

His dark eyes studied her, their intensity never wavering. It felt like he was reading her, as though he could see into the very fabric of her thoughts. She wanted to step back, to put some distance between them, but her legs seemed rooted to the ground, unwilling to move.

"You looked... lost in there," Elijah said, his voice softer now, almost like a whisper. "I thought you might need some air."

Lara's gaze flicked to the night sky, her fingers brushing against the petals of a nearby rose. "I just needed a moment to breathe," she murmured. "It's a lot to take in."

He stepped closer, the faintest sound of his shoes on the gravel barely audible over the wind rustling the leaves. She could feel the heat radiating from him, a warmth that contrasted sharply with the coolness of the night.

"There's a certain kind of energy at these events," Elijah said, his voice now rich with something darker, something deeper. "It's easy to lose yourself in it. To forget who you are."

Lara swallowed, trying to ignore the way his words seemed to settle in her chest like a weight. "And what about you? Do you lose yourself here too?" she asked, half-challenging, half-curious.

His lips quirked in the faintest of smiles, though there was something haunted behind it. "No. I don't lose myself, Lara. I'm always aware of exactly who I am."

The words lingered in the air, heavy with meaning, but before Lara could respond, a gust of wind swept through the courtyard, sending a chill down her spine. She shivered involuntarily, the sudden cold cutting through the thin fabric of her dress. Elijah seemed to notice, his eyes softening, and for a moment, the intensity in his gaze waned.

"Are you cold?" he asked, his voice suddenly gentle, like the touch of a forgotten memory. He reached out, as if to offer her his jacket, but paused, his hand hovering in the air. "You don't have to say yes. But I'd like to help."

The gesture was so simple, and yet it sent a strange ripple through her. She nodded, her throat tight as she whispered, "I'm fine."

But it wasn't fine. The quiet intensity between them was overwhelming, the unspoken tension thickening the air. She could feel the way he was watching her, the weight of his gaze so palpable she could almost taste it. Every movement he made seemed deliberate, as though he was trying to piece together something—something important.

"Lara," Elijah said her name again, and this time, there was an undeniable gravity in the way he said it. "I need to ask you something. And I don't expect an answer right away. But I want you to think about it."

She looked at him, her brow furrowed, her breath still shallow from their earlier dance. "What is it?"

His gaze softened, his voice dropping lower, almost as if he was speaking more to himself than to her. "What if I told you that everything you think you know about yourself is only a small part of the truth? That there's something deeper, something hidden, waiting for you to find it?"

Lara's pulse stuttered in her throat. She wasn't sure how to respond. The words felt too cryptic, too heavy, as though they were laced with something she wasn't ready to understand.

"I don't know what you mean," she said, her voice uncertain, though a flicker of something—dread, curiosity, or maybe both—moved through her.

Elijah's lips parted, but before he could speak, the sound of heels clicking against the stone path interrupted them. A woman's voice, high-pitched and full of false sweetness, called out to Elijah.

"Elijah, darling! There you are."

Lara turned, her heart sinking. The woman approaching them was stunning—tall, with perfectly styled blonde hair and a figure that seemed to belong on the cover of a magazine. She was wearing a dress that glittered in the moonlight, catching the light in a way that seemed almost deliberate. There was something about her—something sharp in the way she moved, like a predator circling her prey.

Lara felt a pang of something deep inside her, an uncomfortable tightening in her chest. She didn't know why, but she felt a rush of jealousy she couldn't explain.

Elijah's expression shifted, the soft intensity fading into something guarded, as though he was a man slipping behind an impenetrable mask. He turned toward the woman, his posture stiffening.

"Helena," he said, his voice cool, but still laced with that same enigmatic edge. "I didn't see you come outside."

"I was just looking for you," Helena purred, her eyes flashing briefly to Lara before returning to Elijah. "I thought we could… catch up."

Lara stood there, rooted to the spot, as the tension between the two of them was palpable. She wanted to leave, to slip away into the night before she had to witness whatever strange dynamic was unfolding between them. But she couldn't move. Her body refused to obey.

Elijah's gaze lingered on Lara for a moment longer, his expression unreadable, before he turned fully to Helena, offering her a polite but distant smile.

"I'm sure you understand, Helena," he said smoothly, "but I was just having a conversation. Perhaps we can talk later."

Helena's lips curled into a tight smile, and for a moment, Lara could see the flicker of something dangerous in her eyes. "Of course, darling. I'll let you finish your… important conversation." Her gaze shot one last, lingering look at Lara before she turned and walked back toward the building.

Lara exhaled slowly, feeling the weight of the silence between her and Elijah. The moment had shifted, and something in the air had changed. The mystery of Elijah deepened, and yet, so did the distance between them.

Elijah turned back to her, his eyes now shadowed, as if the brief interaction had drained him. "I'm sorry," he said quietly, as though the words themselves cost him something. "I didn't mean for this to happen."

Lara blinked, her thoughts swirling. She was torn—torn between wanting to pull away and wanting to stay. "It's fine," she said, her voice steady despite the chaos inside her. "I… I should go."

As she turned to leave, she felt his gaze on her again, as heavy as it was when they first met. But this time, it felt different. This time, it was more than just an invitation to dance. It was a call to something she wasn't sure she could resist.

Something that would change everything.

Three

Shattered Illusions

The rain came suddenly, without warning, as if the sky itself had cracked open in a fit of rage. Lara didn't mind. She welcomed it, the soft thrum of the downpour washing over her like a balm for the lingering unease that clung to her skin. She had spent the better part of the day in the office, a whirlwind of meetings and numbers, but all she could think about was the night before—Elijah.

The tension between them had been undeniable. The electric pull of his gaze, the whispered words he had left her with in the garden, and that soft promise, like a door cracked open, a glimpse into something he wasn't ready to reveal. He had warned her, almost cryptically, that there was more to him than met the eye. And yet, she had still found herself drawn to him, like a moth to a flame, knowing the danger but unwilling to pull away.

Shattered Illusions

But today, as she sat at her desk in the sterile quiet of her office, the events of the night felt like fragments of a dream. Had it really happened? Had she truly danced with Elijah Grayson, spoken to him in such intimate tones, or had it all been some figment of her overactive imagination?

She wasn't sure anymore.

The world outside her window had blurred into a hazy gray, the rain obscuring the view of the bustling city below. Lara stared at the storm, her fingers absently tracing the rim of her coffee mug, her thoughts far from the numbers on her screen. Elijah's face lingered in her mind, a haunting image she couldn't shake. But it wasn't just his presence that consumed her thoughts. It was the way he had looked at her, the way his dark eyes had seemed to peer into her very soul. And then there was that woman—Helena. She didn't know who she was, but the way she had looked at Lara, the way her gaze had lingered with that sharp, knowing edge... it had unsettled her.

It wasn't just jealousy. No, it was something deeper. A feeling that she wasn't the only one caught in a dangerous game. That Elijah, for all his mystery, was just as much a prisoner of forces beyond his control.

And that thought both terrified and intrigued her.

Her phone buzzed on the desk, breaking her from her reverie. She picked it up, her heart giving a slight lurch when she saw the name on the screen. Elijah.

Eclipsed by Your Light

For a moment, she considered not answering, letting it go to voicemail, but something inside her urged her to pick up. She had to know. She had to hear his voice again.

"Lara," his voice crackled through the speaker, low and smooth, as though he had been waiting for her to answer. "I hope I'm not disturbing you."

She swallowed, her breath catching in her throat. His voice had the same effect on her as it had the night before—like a weight on her chest, pulling her into something she wasn't sure she was ready for.

"No," she said, forcing herself to sound casual, to push away the fluttering feeling in her stomach. "Not at all. What's up?"

There was a brief silence on the other end of the line, and for a moment, she wondered if he had second thoughts about calling. But then, his voice returned, soft and hesitant.

"I was hoping I could see you tonight," he said, the words coming out slower than usual, like he was weighing them carefully. "There's something I need to explain. Something... important."

Lara's heart skipped a beat, the weight of his words settling over her like a fog. "Explain?" she echoed, her voice barely above a whisper. "What do you mean?"

"I know I've been distant, Lara. I didn't want to frighten you, but I need to tell you the truth. About me. About why I..." He trailed off, and there was a soft exhale on the other end, like a breath he'd been holding in for far too long. "Please, just meet me. I'll explain everything. I promise."

She hesitated, her thoughts swirling in a chaotic dance of doubt and desire. She wanted to trust him, wanted to believe that there was more to him than the guarded exterior he wore, but something about his request felt urgent, like a thread being pulled, unraveling a tapestry she didn't yet understand.

"I'll be there," she said, the words slipping from her mouth before she could stop them. What was it about him? Why couldn't she just walk away? She was already in too deep, she realized, the path she'd started down was only leading her further into his orbit, and she didn't know how to stop it.

Elijah's voice softened, and for the first time, she detected something raw beneath the cool, controlled façade he always wore. "Thank you," he whispered, and then the line went dead.

Lara sat there for a long moment, staring at the phone in her hand. Her heart was pounding again, the realization that she was stepping into something far darker than she had ever anticipated hitting her like a sudden wave. She couldn't explain it, but the feeling in her gut told her that whatever Elijah was going to tell her, it wasn't going to be easy to hear.

The café they had agreed upon was small and dimly lit, the kind of place that felt like a refuge from the outside world, tucked away from the bustle of the city. Lara arrived early, her mind racing with questions she couldn't seem to quiet. She ordered a cappuccino, fingers tapping nervously on the edge of the table, the sound a harsh contrast to the quiet murmur of conversations around her.

It wasn't long before the door opened, and Elijah stepped inside. The moment he entered, it was as though the entire room shifted, the air around him charged with a presence that was impossible to ignore. He was wearing a dark jacket, the collar turned up against the chill of the evening, and his eyes immediately found hers across the room. There was no hesitation in his gaze, no wavering of emotion. He simply walked toward her, each step purposeful, deliberate, as though he knew exactly where he was going.

Lara stood to greet him, her breath catching in her throat at the intensity of his gaze. He looked different tonight, less guarded, though there was something about his posture that screamed restraint, as though he was holding something back. She couldn't help but wonder if it was fear, or something darker, that kept him tethered in place.

"Lara," he said her name like a prayer, his voice a velvet whisper that made her skin tingle. "I'm glad you came."

She nodded, feeling the heat of his gaze as he sat down across from her. "You said you had something to explain," she said, her voice steady despite the fluttering in her chest. "What's going on, Elijah?"

For a moment, he didn't answer. Instead, he looked down at his hands, fidgeting with the sleeve of his jacket as if the words he needed to say were caught in his throat. Lara waited, her heart thudding loudly in her ears. She could feel the tension between them, like a wire stretched taut, waiting to snap.

Finally, he looked up, and when his eyes met hers, they were darker than she had ever seen them—empty, haunted. "I've been running from the truth for a long time, Lara," he said, his voice low and strained. "And I've been trying to protect you from it. But I can't keep hiding."

Lara leaned forward, the weight of his words pressing down on her. "What truth?" she asked, her voice barely a whisper.

Elijah exhaled slowly, his eyes flickering toward the window before returning to her. "There's something you don't know about me. Something that could change everything."

Her heart thudded in her chest, each beat reverberating like the sound of a drum in the quiet café. Whatever this was, whatever he was about to reveal, she wasn't prepared for it. And yet, part of her knew she was already in too deep to back away now.

He opened his mouth to speak, but before he could, a shadow crossed the table. A figure—a woman—loomed over them. Her eyes, dark and sharp as glass, locked onto Lara's with a gaze so cold it felt like a knife pressing into her chest.

"I think it's time we had a conversation," the woman said, her voice smooth but laced with malice.

Four

The Mask Beneath

The café door slammed open with a gust of wind that sent a chill through Lara's bones. The woman who had appeared at their table—the one with the cold, calculating eyes—stood there for a moment as if she were waiting for the storm to settle before she approached. She was tall, impossibly slender, dand raped in a dark, form-fitting coat that made her appear almost ethereal in the dim light of the café. Her hair was a striking shade of platinum blonde, swept back into an elegant chignon. She looked every bit the picture of refined beauty, but there was something in her eyes—something sharp, as though she had been carved from ice rather than born from it.

Lara's heart skipped a beat. Her instinct was to stand up, to leave this café that had suddenly transformed into an arena of tension, but she couldn't tear her eyes away from the woman

The Mask Beneath

who stood before them. The sudden, suffocating atmosphere weighed heavily on her chest, but she couldn't escape it.

Elijah's face had gone rigid. His usual calm demeanor seemed to fracture under the woman's presence, his eyes darting between her and Lara, a flash of something like regret—or fear?—flickering behind the mask he wore so carefully.

"Helena," he said, his voice strained, barely above a whisper. The name was like a dark secret on his tongue, one he had never intended to reveal.

The woman—Helena—stared at him, her lips curling into a smile that never reached her eyes. "You should've known I'd find you, Elijah. You can't run forever." Her voice was cold, smooth, and polished, like fine china, but there was something venomous beneath it.

Lara's pulse quickened as she watched the exchange. Something about the way they looked at each other—the way their gazes locked—felt intimate in the most unsettling way. It was clear that this was more than just a mere acquaintance. Their history was deep, tangled, and there was a darkness to it that neither was willing to reveal.

"What do you want, Helena?" Elijah's words were clipped, each one spoken with the effort of restraint, as if the act of even acknowledging her presence was a burden. "I've told you, I'm done with all of this."

Helena's gaze shifted to Lara, her eyes narrowing slightly, as if sizing her up. "You're done, Elijah? Is that why you've been avoiding me? Is that why you've been parading your little... distraction in front of me?" Her tone was sharp, cutting through the air like a blade. Lara felt her cheeks flush with a heat she couldn't explain—resentment, shame, or something else altogether—but it was there, simmering beneath the surface.

Lara opened her mouth to respond, but the words stuck in her throat. Her instincts screamed at her to stand up and leave, to escape this suffocating encounter, but she couldn't. She was frozen, a part of her mesmerized by the tension that crackled between Elijah and this woman—Helena.

Elijah's gaze snapped back to her, and for a fleeting moment, Lara saw something break through the layers of his carefully constructed walls—something raw, something real. His eyes softened, a flicker of vulnerability showing through the cracks.

"Lara," he said, his voice gentle, almost apologetic. "This is... Helena. She's someone from my past. Someone I should've left behind long ago." He paused, his voice catching slightly, like a dam on the verge of breaking. "But she's not someone I can easily escape."

Helena's lips twisted into something almost like amusement as she watched Elijah's discomfort. "Is that so?" she asked, her voice dripping with false sweetness. "Well, Elijah, it's been lovely catching up. But I think it's time for you to come back to the real world. You can't hide forever."

Lara's breath caught in her throat as Helena's eyes flicked

The Mask Beneath

back to her once more. There was something in the woman's gaze—something calculated—that sent a shiver down her spine. Helena wasn't just here to talk; she was here to claim Elijah. And Lara, standing in the middle of it, was little more than an obstacle to be eliminated.

The air between them grew thick with unspoken tension, the space around them humming with the weight of unresolved history. Lara could feel the heat rising in her chest, her thoughts spinning in a frenzy. She wanted to scream, to demand answers, but the words wouldn't come.

Elijah was still looking at her, his eyes pleading for something—understanding, maybe? But it was hard to focus on him when Helena's presence loomed over them like a storm cloud. The woman exuded power, a quiet dominance that was impossible to ignore. It was clear that Elijah was caught between them, trapped in some kind of unholy bond that had lasted far longer than it should have.

"I'm not going anywhere, Elijah," Helena continued, her voice low and insistent. "You're coming with me, whether you like it or not."

Elijah's jaw tightened, his hand balling into a fist on the table, but he didn't move. The vulnerability that had flashed across his face was gone, replaced by a mask of cold indifference. Lara noticed the subtle shift in his demeanor—the way he pulled back, as if retreating into himself, closing off the world around him.

"I don't belong with you, Helena," he said, his words harsh, but the undercurrent of sadness in his voice couldn't be hidden. "Not anymore."

Helena's lips twisted into a smile that was more of a sneer than anything else. "You think you can just walk away from me, from what we have? You're not the same man I used to know, Elijah. You never were."

Lara's pulse raced as she watched the scene unfold before her. Every word, every glance, seemed to carry more weight than she could comprehend. She felt like an outsider, caught in a web of emotions and secrets that didn't belong to her, yet she couldn't tear herself away.

For a moment, the tension in the air was palpable, almost suffocating. Helena was waiting for something—for Elijah to give in, to acknowledge her control over him. But Elijah didn't move. He didn't give her that satisfaction.

"I'm not going anywhere with you, Helena," he said again, his voice stronger now, but still filled with the underlying sorrow of someone who had long ago given up fighting for freedom.

The silence that followed was deafening. Lara could hear the soft clink of cups from the other tables, the rustling of paper as a nearby customer flipped through a menu, but it all felt distant, muffled by the storm brewing between the three of them.

Helena's gaze never left Elijah, but there was something in the way her eyes flicked to Lara that made Lara's skin prickle.

She could feel the weight of the woman's disdain, the silent challenge that passed between them. Helena wasn't just here to reclaim Elijah—she was here to prove a point.

Elijah stood up suddenly, his chair scraping loudly against the floor. "I'm leaving," he said firmly, his tone brokering no argument. His eyes met Lara's one last time, the briefest flicker of something unreadable crossing his face. "Come with me," he whispered.

The words were like a lifeline thrown to her, but Lara hesitated. The pull between them was undeniable, a magnetic force she couldn't ignore, but she wasn't sure if she was ready for whatever this was. Whatever he was.

But before she could make up her mind, Helena's voice sliced through the air, cold and final.

"If you think you can just walk away from everything, Elijah, you're wrong. You can't escape this. Not anymore."

Lara felt a shudder run through her at the venom in Helena's voice. It was clear now that whatever bond had existed between her and Elijah was far darker than either of them were willing to admit. And Lara was trapped in the middle, uncertain of where her place was, or if she even had one.

As Elijah turned toward the door, Lara stood, her legs trembling beneath her. The café had become a battleground, and she was standing in the crossfire. Every part of her wanted to run, to find the safety of her apartment, where nothing—no one—could threaten the fragile illusion of peace she had built. But something inside her refused to back down. There was a connection between her and Elijah, something too powerful to ignore.

And as they stepped out into the cold night, with Helena's shadow still looming over them, Lara knew—no matter how much she wanted to escape, there was no turning back now.

Five

Into the Abyss

The rain had slowed to a drizzle, leaving the world around them soaked and heavy with the scent of wet earth. The streets glistened under the lamplight, reflecting the pale glow like a mirror, but Lara didn't notice. She barely noticed anything beyond the man at her side, his presence a constant pull that seemed to magnetize every part of her. Elijah walked ahead of her, his steps deliberate, cutting through the mist that clung to the city's skin like an unwanted memory.

Lara's heart pounded in her chest, the aftershock of Helena's confrontation still reverberating in the space between them. It wasn't just Helena's icy demeanor or her sharp, accusatory words that lingered in the air. It was Elijah—his strained silence, the tension in his jaw, the way he seemed to be carrying the weight of a thousand unspoken thoughts. She could feel the heaviness of it, a pressure in her own chest, but he didn't look at her. Not once, not since they'd stepped out of the café, as if he was closing himself off from her, from everything.

The city was quiet, save for the occasional car passing by, the faint hum of distant voices filtering through the night. It felt like they were alone in a world of shadows, the streetlights casting long, distorted shapes on the pavement as they walked. She could hear Elijah's breathing, low and steady, like he was preparing himself for something, but what? She couldn't shake the sense that he was on the verge of something, something he wasn't ready to share but couldn't hide forever.

"Elijah," she said, her voice small against the vastness of the night. Her feet seemed to move on their own, carrying her closer to him, but when she reached out to touch his arm, he flinched as if her hand were a blade instead of comfort. The gesture sent a jolt of pain through her, a crack in the fragile wall she'd started to build around her heart.

He stopped abruptly, turning to face her, his eyes dark and unreadable. There was a flicker of something behind them, a storm waiting to break. He stood there for a moment, his shoulders tense, like a man at war with himself.

"I didn't want you to be part of this, Lara," Elijah's voice was tight, as though every word cost him something. "You don't know what you're walking into."

The words hit her like a slap, the coldness of them sinking into her skin. She stepped back, her eyes narrowing as she tried to make sense of them. "What does that mean? What do you mean by this?" she demanded, the frustration building in her chest. "You said you wanted to be rid of her, but you don't look rid of her, Elijah. You look... trapped. Like there's something you're not telling me."

He hesitated, the flickering light from the lamppost casting shadows over his face, making his expression harder to read. He didn't say anything, just stared at her with a mixture of apology and pain that made her want to step forward and close the distance between them. But she didn't.

"I'm not trapped," he said, his voice a little softer now, though still carrying that underlying tension. "Not anymore."

But the words felt hollow. The same words he had said before, with Helena—I'm done. And yet, the unspoken history between him and the woman still hung over him like a cloud, casting a shadow over every word. She could see it now—the cracks in his carefully crafted persona. He wasn't as unshakable as he pretended to be. There was something deeper, darker beneath the surface, and for the first time, Lara realized she might not want to know what it was.

Elijah took a step toward her, his eyes not leaving hers. "Lara, you don't understand. What Helena is to me... it's not simple. It never was." His voice dropped to a whisper. "I thought I could outrun it. I thought I could outrun her. But I can't. I never could."

There it was again—the quiet confession, the vulnerability he couldn't hide, the rawness in his words that stripped away the layers of mystery. Lara's heart ached at the realization. He was drowning, and she was standing at the edge of the abyss, unsure whether to reach out and pull him to safety or step back and let him fall.

"I don't need you to fix me," he added, the words sharp, but his eyes were pleading. "I never asked for you to get involved."

She flinched at that. He didn't want her here. She could hear it in his voice, in the space between the words, the coldness that clung to them like frost. She stepped back, the sting of his rejection cutting deeper than she expected. "Then why did you call me?" The question slipped from her lips before she could stop it, her voice barely above a whisper, vulnerable, raw.

His eyes softened, just a little, and for a moment, the walls seemed to crack open. "Because I couldn't keep you away," he said, his voice almost tender, but there was a bitter edge to it. "Because you're the only thing that's felt real in a long time, Lara. And I'm scared. I'm scared of what will happen if I let myself need you too much."

Lara's chest tightened at the admission, the confession hanging in the air like a delicate thread between them. She wanted to reach out to him, to close the distance and hold him, to reassure him that everything would be okay. But she couldn't. She didn't know if she could fix whatever was broken inside of him.

There was a long silence, the kind that made every breath feel like an eternity. She looked at him, really looked at him, and make sense of them. "What does that mean? What do you mean by this?" she demanded, the frustration building in her chest. "You said you wanted to be rid of her, but you don't look rid of her, Elijah. You look... trapped. Like there's something you're not telling me."

He hesitated, the flickering light from the lamppost casting shadows over his face, making his expression harder to read. He didn't say anything, just stared at her with a mixture of apology and pain that made her want to step forward and close the distance between them. But she didn't.

"I'm not trapped," he said, his voice a little softer now, though still carrying that underlying tension. "Not anymore."

But the words felt hollow. The same words he had said before, with Helena—I'm done. And yet, the unspoken history between him and the woman still hung over him like a cloud, casting a shadow over every word. She could see it now—the cracks in his carefully crafted persona. He wasn't as unshakable as he pretended to be. There was something deeper, darker beneath the surface, and for the first time, Lara realized she might not want to know what it was.

Elijah took a step toward her, his eyes not leaving hers. "Lara, you don't understand. What Helena is to me... it's not simple. It never was." His voice dropped to a whisper. "I thought I could outrun it. I thought I could outrun her. But I can't. I never could."

There it was again—the quiet confession, the vulnerability he couldn't hide, the rawness in his words that stripped away the layers of mystery. Lara's heart ached at the realization. He was drowning, and she was standing at the edge of the abyss, unsure whether to reach out and pull him to safety or step back and let him fall.

"I don't need you to fix me," he added, the words sharp, but his eyes were pleading. "I never asked for you to get involved."

She flinched at that. He didn't want her here. She could hear it in his voice, in the space between the words, the coldness that clung to them like frost. She stepped back, the sting of his rejection cutting deeper than she expected. "Then why did you call me?" The question slipped from her lips before she could stop it, her voice barely above a whisper, vulnerable, raw.

His eyes softened, just a little, and for a moment, the walls seemed to crack open. "Because I couldn't keep you away," he said, his voice almost tender, but there was a bitter edge to it. "Because you're the only thing that's felt real in a long time, Lara. And I'm scared. I'm scared of what will happen if I let myself need you too much."

Lara's chest tightened at the admission, the confession hanging in the air like a delicate thread between them. She wanted to reach out to him, to close the distance and hold him, to reassure him that everything would be okay. But she couldn't. She didn't know if she could fix whatever was broken inside of him.

There was a long silence, the kind that made every breath feel like an eternity. She looked at him, really looked at him, and saw the cracks, the lies he had been telling himself, the fear that haunted his every step.

"I can't save you from this," she said, the words thick in her throat. "I can't fix you, Elijah. You have to do that on your own."

He seemed to take the words in, his jaw tightening as if he were swallowing them down. His eyes never left hers, though they seemed to be seeing something else, something far beyond her. Something painful. "I know," he said softly. "I know."

But even as he said it, she saw the way his eyes darted to the alley behind her, the way his body stiffened, as though he were waiting for something, or someone. She glanced over her shoulder, but the alley was empty, cloaked in shadows. Still, the feeling in the pit of her stomach didn't fade. It only deepened.

"Lara," Elijah said, his voice low, a warning lacing his tone. "Go. You shouldn't be here."

She shook her head, a lump forming in her throat. "I'm not leaving you like this, Elijah. You can't just push me away. I won't—"

Before she could finish, a figure stepped out from the shadows behind them. The hair on the back of her neck stood on end as the man's silhouette took shape in the dim light. Lara's breath caught in her throat as she recognized the familiar face, though it was twisted in a way she hadn't expected. Dark eyes, framed by a scar that ran down his cheek. The man was older, but there was no mistaking who he was.

"Don't turn around, Lara," Elijah murmured, his voice tight, a thread of panic running through it. "Please."

But it was too late.

The man stepped forward, his smile cold and calculating, eyes gleaming with something dangerous. "You're still running, Elijah?" the man said, his voice grating like gravel. "You've never been good at running. And now you've dragged someone else into your mess. That was a mistake."

Lara felt a chill creep over her skin. Her mind raced, trying to piece together the puzzle, but everything felt too fast, too sharp. Elijah's warning, the look of panic in his eyes—it was clear now that this wasn't just about Helena. This man was part of the reason Elijah was running.

"Who are you?" she demanded, her voice trembling despite herself. Her body was on edge, every instinct telling her to run, but she couldn't tear her eyes away from the scene before her.

The man chuckled darkly. "Oh, sweet girl, you really don't know, do you?" He stepped closer, his presence pressing down on her like a vice. "My name is Victor. And I'm the reason Elijah can't escape."

Lara's heart pounded in her chest, the words sinking deep into her bones. She had no idea what she had stepped into, but there was no way out now. Not without Elijah. And Elijah was already so far gone, lost in a world darker than she had ever imagined.

Six

The Whispering Shadows

The air in the small, dimly lit apartment was thick with tension, the silence between Lara and Elijah more suffocating than the heavy summer night outside. The faint hum of the city drifted in through the cracked window, but it felt distant, as if the world outside had been muted, leaving only the two of them in the quiet aftermath of everything that had just happened.

Lara sat on the edge of the worn couch, her legs tucked underneath her, her hands gripping the fabric of her dress so tightly that her knuckles had turned white. Elijah, standing near the window, seemed like a ghost, his figure half-lit by the streetlight outside, the shadows cast across his face making it impossible to read his expression. His back was rigid, his shoulders tense, and for the first time since she had met him, Lara felt the full weight of the distance between them.

The Whispering Shadows

Victor's presence, the way he had stepped into their lives with a cold smile and a look that suggested a long, shared history, had shattered something between her and Elijah. The man's words had hung in the air like a dark promise: I'm the reason Elijah can't escape. That had been enough to make everything Lara thought she knew feel like a lie. But she still didn't understand it all—not the depth of Elijah's ties to Victor, not the way Helena fit into this tangled web of shadows.

And yet, even now, with the weight of Victor's words and the overwhelming uncertainty gnawing at her insides, all Lara could think about was Elijah. His silence was a wall, one she couldn't scale, no matter how hard she tried.

"You should go," Elijah said suddenly, his voice low and rough, like it hadn't been used in hours. His words cut through the quiet like a knife, sharp and definitive.

Lara flinched at the coldness in his tone, the finality in it. She stood up quickly, her body moving of its own accord, but her mind felt sluggish, paralyzed by the sudden shift in him. She could feel the heat of the space between them, the pulsing distance that seemed to expand with every passing second.

"Go?" she repeated, her voice trembling slightly despite her best efforts to sound composed. "Elijah, what do you mean? After everything, you want me to just leave?"

He didn't turn to look at her, but she could feel his gaze, heavy and distant, even from where she stood. She could see the tension in his back, the way his body seemed to carry a weight too heavy to share. His fingers gripped the windowsill, the muscles in his forearms straining as if the simple act of holding onto the frame was taking every ounce of strength he had left.

"You don't understand," he said, the words so low, they were almost lost in the quiet of the room. His voice was strained, taut with something she couldn't name—guilt, perhaps, or fear. But it wasn't just that. It was something darker, something buried so deep inside of him that she couldn't begin to unravel it.

Lara took a step toward him, her heart hammering in her chest. "No, I don't understand. But I want to. I need to know what's going on, Elijah. I can't… I can't just walk away from you."

His body tensed at her words, and for the briefest moment, she saw something flicker across his face. Something that told her he wasn't as closed off as he seemed. Something that made her heart ache with the need to reach him, to break through whatever it was that was locking him away.

But before she could take another step toward him, the door to the apartment creaked open, and a figure appeared in the doorway. Lara's breath caught in her throat, her body instinctively recoiling from the sight of the man standing there. Victor.

He looked the same as before—cold, imposing, his presence filling the doorway like a storm cloud blocking out the light. His eyes gleamed with something that made Lara's skin prickle, something too knowing, too dangerous. She felt an overwhelming sense of unease wash over her, her instincts screaming for her to leave, to run.

But Elijah didn't flinch. He didn't even look at the man.

"I thought you'd be gone by now," Victor said, his voice smooth, almost too casual. He stepped fully into the apartment, closing the door behind him with a soft click. "But I see you're still here. I must have underestimated your persistence, Elijah."

Lara swallowed the lump in her throat, the fear rising like a wave threatening to pull her under. She didn't know who this man was, not really. But she knew that he was trouble, and not just the kind that could be swept away with a few words. No, this was something much darker.

"Elijah," she said, her voice barely above a whisper. She didn't know what else to say. She didn't know how to make sense of this man, of this situation. "Who is he?"

Victor's laugh, low and cruel, echoed in the small room, sending a shiver down Lara's spine. "Who am I?" he repeated, his gaze flicking between them. "Well, I suppose I'm the one who's been keeping Elijah here all these years. The one who's been keeping him from you, sweet girl."

Lara's heart skipped a beat. "What do you mean?" she asked, her voice hoarse. "What are you talking about?"

Victor's eyes gleamed as he stepped closer, closing the gap between them, his presence suffocating. "You think it's all just about Helena?" He tilted his head, his smile widening, as if enjoying the game he was playing. "No. It's bigger than that. Elijah's been part of something… much more dangerous. Something that doesn't just let people walk away. It traps them."

Lara's stomach dropped, the blood rushing from her head as the full weight of Victor's words hit her. Traps them. She could feel the coldness in the pit of her stomach, the fear creeping in, its icy fingers tightening around her chest. She looked at Elijah, but he wouldn't meet her gaze. His face was a mask, but his eyes… His eyes were haunted.

"Stop," Elijah said suddenly, his voice raw, the words cutting through the tension like a knife. He turned to face Victor, finally locking eyes with him. "Stop playing with her."

Victor raised an eyebrow, the amusement in his eyes turning into something sharper, more dangerous. "Playing with her?" he repeated, his voice mocking. "I'm not playing, Elijah. I'm just telling her the truth. She deserves to know."

Lara's breath hitched in her chest, her mind racing to catch up with the conversation. "The truth about what?" she demanded, her voice more forceful now. "What's going on, Elijah? Tell me the truth."

Elijah's eyes finally found hers, and for the first time in what felt like an eternity, she saw something in them—a flicker of the man she had been growing closer to, the man she had started to believe in. He looked at her like he was about to say something, like the weight of everything was crashing down on him and he couldn't hold it in anymore. But then, something changed.

The Whispering Shadows

A shadow crossed his face, and he looked away.

"I can't, Lara," he whispered, his voice shaking with the effort of holding back whatever it was he wanted to say. "I can't do this to you."

Victor's laugh rang out again, sharp and triumphant. "Too late for that," he said, his voice a low rumble. "You're already in this, sweetheart. And you won't get out until Elijah faces the consequences of his past. Until we all face them."

Lara's mind was spinning. Her heart was in her throat, and the room felt like it was closing in on her. She couldn't breathe, couldn't think. Everything she thought she knew was falling apart in front of her, unraveling like a thread she couldn't control.

Victor stepped forward, his eyes never leaving hers, and his words felt like an icy dagger to the heart. "You're part of this now, Lara," he said softly, almost tenderly. "Whether Elijah wants you to be or not."

The darkness in his voice, the cold certainty of his words, froze her in place. And in that moment, as she looked at Elijah—standing there, torn between the man he had been and the man he had become—Lara realized something. She wasn't just in danger of losing Elijah. She was in danger of losing herself in the shadows he had brought with him.

Seven

Secrets in the Bloodline

The apartment felt smaller than it ever had before. Once familiar and comforting, the walls now closed in on Lara, each one a silent witness to the chaos swirling around her. The air was thick, weighed down by unspoken truths and the suffocating tension between Elijah and the shadow of his past. She could feel it—the dark thread running through everything. It was in the way Victor had spoken of Elijah's past, of things unsaid that lingered in the space between them. It was in the way Elijah's silence spoke volumes, the walls around him growing higher with each passing second.

Lara sat on the edge of the couch, her hands folded tightly in her lap, her fingers trembling slightly. The room was dim, the only light coming from the single lamp near the window, casting long shadows across the walls. The muffled hum of the city outside seeped through the cracked window, a reminder of the life she once thought was hers. But that life felt like a distant memory now, a life that had been swept away by the tidal wave of secrets Elijah had yet to share.

She looked over at him, sitting across from her, his eyes distant, focused on something she couldn't see. His face was drawn, pale in the weak light, the lines of stress etched deeper than before. There was something broken in him now, something she hadn't noticed before, something she wasn't sure how to fix—or if it could be fixed at all.

"Elijah," she said, her voice breaking the heavy silence that had settled between them like dust. "You have to tell me what's going on. I can't do this anymore. I need to know what you're hiding."

His eyes flickered to hers, a flash of something—regret, pain, fear?—crossing his face before he masked it again. The moment was fleeting, but it was enough to send a shiver down her spine. He opened his mouth as if to speak, but no words came out. Instead, he ran a hand through his dark hair, a gesture of frustration, before finally speaking, his voice hoarse.

"I'm sorry, Lara," he whispered, his gaze dropping to the floor. "I never meant for you to get involved in this. I never wanted to pull you into my mess."

Lara stood, unable to sit still any longer. Her chest tightened with a mixture of confusion and hurt. "But you did, Elijah. I'm already involved. I have been since the first night we met. I'm not going anywhere until you tell me the truth."

He was silent for a long moment, the weight of her words hanging in the air like a storm cloud waiting to burst. When he finally spoke, his voice was barely audible, as if he were afraid to say the words aloud.

"There's something in my bloodline, Lara. Something that's been passed down for generations. A curse." The words sounded impossible, too heavy to bear, but they fell from his lips like a secret he could no longer keep.

Lara felt her breath catch in her throat. "A curse?" she repeated, the disbelief clear in her voice. "Elijah, you can't be serious. A curse? That sounds like—"

"Like a fairy tale?" he finished for her, his voice bitter. He looked up, locking eyes with her. "I wish it were. But it's real, Lara. It's part of who I am. It's part of who we are."

Lara took a step forward, her mind reeling from the revelation. She had known there was something more to Elijah's past, something dark and hidden, but this… this was beyond anything she had imagined. "What do you mean, 'we'?" she asked, her voice trembling.

Elijah exhaled sharply, his eyes closing as if the weight of the confession was too much to bear. "My family… the Graysons. We've been tied to this curse for generations. It's in our blood, Lara. It's why we can't leave. It's why we can't be free."

Lara's mind raced, her thoughts spinning out of control as the pieces of the puzzle began to shift into place. "How does it work? What's the curse?" she asked, her voice barely a whisper, the urgency in her words cutting through the thick silence of the room.

Elijah met her gaze, his expression pained, as if the words were tearing him apart. "The Grayson bloodline is tied to something ancient, something older than us. It's tied to power, to forces beyond our control. We're bound by a pact—an oath made long ago. The curse keeps us tethered to the past, to things we can't escape."

Lara's stomach dropped. The way he said it, the weight in his voice—it felt real, like a cold truth that couldn't be denied. "What kind of power? What pact?" she asked, her voice cracking with the desperation she felt.

"Elijah's father was a part of it," came a voice from the doorway, low and menacing. Lara turned sharply, her heart skipping a beat as she saw Helena standing in the frame. She hadn't heard her come in, hadn't even sensed her presence. The woman was like a shadow, slipping in and out of rooms unnoticed, her face a mask of cold calculation.

Lara's pulse quickened. "Helena," she said, her voice strained with the tension that crackled in the room. "What do you know about this? About the curse?"

Helena stepped fully into the room, her gaze flickering between the two of them. "Everything, Lara," she said, her voice smooth, yet laced with something dangerous. "I know everything about the Grayson family. And I know that Elijah's father was the one who made the pact. The one who sealed the curse."

Lara's mind spun as she took in the new information. "What kind of pact? What was the price?" she demanded, her heart racing.

Helena looked at Elijah with a glint in her eye, as if she were savoring the moment. "The price was always the same. A sacrifice. A life. And every generation after that has had to pay."

Lara's legs almost gave out beneath her. She could feel the blood drain from her face as the words settled in her mind. "A sacrifice?" she repeated, her voice hollow. "Who… who had to die?"

Helena's smile was cold, almost triumphant. "Someone in the Grayson family had to die every time the pact was renewed. And now, Elijah is next."

Lara felt the ground shift beneath her feet. The realization hit her like a physical blow, the weight of it pressing down on her chest. She looked at Elijah, but he wasn't meeting her gaze. His eyes were closed, his jaw clenched in a grimace of pain. He knew. He had known all along, and now it was too late. She was too deep in it. They were both too deep.

"You're telling me," Lara began, her voice unsteady, "that you've known this your entire life? That your family's been killing each other to keep this curse alive?"

Elijah opened his eyes then, meeting her gaze, and there was a deep sadness in them—an ocean of pain that she wasn't sure she could ever understand. "It's not that simple, Lara," he whispered. "I didn't choose this. None of us did. But it's part of who we are. It's a legacy that we can't escape."

Lara could feel the tears threatening to spill, the weight of everything crashing down on her all at once. She wanted to scream, to run, to get as far away from this nightmare as possible. But there was nowhere to run. Not anymore.

"Helena," she said, her voice trembling with anger and fear. "What do you want? Why are you here?"

Helena's eyes gleamed with something dark, something predatory. "I'm here because the time is near, Lara. The pact is about to be renewed. And whether Elijah likes it or not, he has to fulfill his part. He has to make the sacrifice."

Lara's heart stopped. She looked at Elijah, her mind reeling, trying to understand what Helena was saying. "What are you talking about?" she asked, her voice barely a whisper. "Who... who are you talking about? What sacrifice?"

Helena's smile was like ice. "You, Lara," she said softly, her voice carrying a sense of finality. "You are the sacrifice."

Everything inside Lara froze. Her blood turned to ice, her limbs heavy with shock. She couldn't breathe. She couldn't think. The words echoed in her ears, too much to process, too horrifying to believe.

But Elijah's eyes were fixed on hers now, and there was no mistaking the pain in them. No mistaking the guilt that had been building between them since the moment they met. He hadn't wanted this. He hadn't wanted her to be part of this curse. But there was no way out. There was no escaping it.

"You can't…" Lara's voice faltered, but she could feel the truth in the air, the suffocating weight of it.

"You will," Helena said, her voice low and final, as the truth of the curse settled into the room like a shadow.

Eight

Unraveling Threads

The moon hung high in the sky, a silver sentinel above the city, its light spilling through the cracks of the blinds, casting long shadows across the room. Lara sat at the edge of the bed, her legs drawn tightly to her chest, her fingers clutching the fabric of the blanket. The night felt alive, suffocating, as though it were pressing in on her, leaving her no escape. Everything she thought she knew about Elijah, about herself, had been twisted, bent into something darker, something dangerous.

Her mind refused to stop. Every piece of information, every word that had been spoken in the last twenty-four hours, seemed to replay over and over again, like a broken record, each repetition driving the pain deeper into her chest. She could still hear Helena's voice in her ears, her words laced with cruelty, the cold promise that Lara was the sacrifice. And worse still, she could see the look in Elijah's eyes when the truth had finally come to light. He hadn't wanted this. He hadn't wanted her to be a part of it. But he hadn't fought for her, either. He had let her step into the storm, and now they were both trapped in its eye.

The apartment was eerily quiet now, the soft hum of the city below the only sound to fill the stillness. Elijah had left hours ago, after the confrontation with Helena. He hadn't said much before he walked out, just a brief, almost apologetic glance before he closed the door behind him, leaving her alone in the oppressive silence of the room.

Lara squeezed her eyes shut, trying to push the thoughts away. She couldn't afford to think about it—not yet. But the knot in her stomach tightened with each passing second, the fear building inside her, threatening to choke her. She had to do something. She had to find a way to stop this—to stop whatever was about to happen.

Her thoughts were interrupted by a soft knock on the door. She froze. It wasn't the usual gentle tap of a visitor—this was more like a whisper, quiet and insistent. Her pulse quickened, and her breath caught in her throat. She hadn't expected anyone. Elijah hadn't said anything about returning, and the thought of facing him again, after everything, was almost too much to bear. But something told her this wasn't him. It couldn't be.

She stood up, her legs shaky as she crossed the room toward the door. She hesitated for a moment, her hand hovering just above the doorknob, before she turned it and pulled the door open.

The man standing on the other side wasn't Elijah. He wasn't even someone she recognized. His face was sharp, angular, with dark eyes that held an unsettling amount of knowledge. His features were unreadable, though there was an air of quiet menace about him, something that made her instinctively take a step back.

"Lara Whitaker?" His voice was low, calm, almost too calm. It sent a shiver down her spine, like the soft rustling of leaves before a storm.

"Yes," she replied, her voice tight. She wanted to slam the door shut, to run, to hide from whatever this man represented, but she stood frozen, caught in his gaze.

"I'm here to talk to you about Elijah," he said, his words slow, deliberate, as if he were savoring them. "And about the path you've walked into."

Lara's heart skipped a beat. This wasn't a chance encounter. This was deliberate. And it made her stomach twist with an icy dread. "What do you want with him?" she demanded, trying to sound braver than she felt. "And why are you here?"

The man smiled, a smile that didn't reach his eyes. "You don't understand, do you? Elijah's already in too deep. The question isn't what we want with him—it's what we want with you."

Lara took a step back, the hairs on her neck standing on end.

We. She hadn't seen any hint of a group, a larger presence, but this man's words hung in the air like a threat, a suggestion that things were much worse than she had imagined.

"I don't know who you are," she said, her voice shaking despite her best efforts. "And I don't want to."

The man's eyes flickered with something dangerous, but he didn't move. "I'm someone who's been watching over Elijah for a long time. Keeping an eye on things. We've been… waiting. And now you're part of it."

Lara's mind raced, her heart hammering in her chest as the room seemed to close in on her. "You're part of this curse, aren't you?" she asked, the words slipping out before she could stop them.

The man didn't answer right away. Instead, he tilted his head slightly, as if considering her question. "The curse is only part of it," he said finally, his voice dripping with something darker than she could put into words. "It's the price we all pay. Elijah's father made sure of that. But you, Lara, you have a role to play, too. A bigger one than you realize."

Lara's stomach dropped, a cold sweat breaking out on the back of her neck. She could feel the walls of the apartment closing in, the weight of the man's words pressing on her chest. She wanted to run. She wanted to escape. But she couldn't. Not anymore.

"What do you want from me?" she asked, her voice barely above a whisper.

The man's smile widened, though it held no warmth, no trace of kindness. "We want you to understand, Lara. We want you to accept what's coming. And we want you to make a choice."

Her heart pounded in her ears, her breath coming in shallow gasps. "What choice?" she asked, though she already knew the answer. She could feel it, like a dark shadow hovering over her, just out of reach.

"Whether you're willing to make the same sacrifice," he said, stepping closer, his presence filling the doorway. "Whether you're ready to save Elijah by giving up what's most precious to you."

Lara's knees almost gave way beneath her. The man's words were like a weight pressing down on her chest, suffocating her. She wanted to scream, to fight back, but her voice wouldn't come. The idea of sacrificing anything, of losing herself to this curse, was too much to bear.

"Why me?" she whispered, her voice shaking with the fear that was starting to settle in her bones. "Why is it me?"

The man's expression softened, just slightly, as if he were savoring the fear in her voice. "Because you're the key, Lara. You're the one who can break the cycle. But only if you understand what it takes to do it."

Lara stared at him, her mind reeling, struggling to comprehend the gravity of what he was saying. She wanted to push him away, slam the door, scream for help—but she didn't know who to turn to. She was alone in this. Alone with Elijah, trapped in a web that seemed to get tighter with every passing second.

"You're playing with fire," she said finally, her voice hoarse. "You don't know what you're asking of me."

The man's eyes flickered with something close to amusement. "Oh, I know exactly what I'm asking. And you'll understand soon enough. Whether you want to or not."

Before Lara could respond, he turned and walked away, his footsteps echoing in the silence of the hallway. She stood frozen in the doorway, staring at the empty space where he had been, her mind a whirlwind of questions, of fear, and of a terrible, awful understanding.

The air in the room seemed to close in around her, the weight of everything pressing down on her chest. She couldn't breathe. She couldn't think. Everything had shifted, and there was no going back now.

And the worst part? She was already part of the curse. She was already tangled in its threads, whether she wanted to be or not.

She had to make a choice. A choice she wasn't sure she could live with.

Her heart ached, the words of the man still ringing in her ears. There was no escaping it, no running away. She had already walked too far into the abyss. And now, she had to decide whether to embrace the darkness or burn alongside it.

Nine

The Heart of Darkness

The night had deepened, swallowing the city in shadows, and the air felt heavier with each breath Lara took. The apartment was suffocating now, its walls pressing in from every direction. She could still feel the man's presence lingering in the doorway, the chill of his words, his warnings, curling around her like a poison she couldn't shake. Every part of her screamed for escape, for some way out of this nightmare, but every path seemed to lead deeper into the dark heart of the storm.

She had thought she was ready for the truth. She had thought she could face whatever Elijah had been hiding, whatever his family's cursed bloodline entailed. But now, with each passing moment, the weight of it all crushed her. The threat of the curse, the terrifying unknown that loomed over them like a predator waiting to strike, was closing in on her with an inevitability she couldn't outrun.

Her mind kept circling back to that moment—when the man had spoken about sacrifice. *You're the key*, he had said. *You're the one who can break the cycle. But only if you understand what it takes to do it.*

The choice. The horrible, impossible choice.

Lara stood near the window now, her fingers pressed to the cool glass, looking out at the city below. The streets were still bustling with life, but to her, it all felt far away, as if she were watching the world through a fogged lens. She had been a part of this world, and yet, she no longer recognized it. Every step, every decision, had led her here, to this point of no return.

The door opened behind her, the soft click of the latch echoing through the room. Elijah stepped inside, his presence filling the space with a heavy silence. He didn't say anything at first. He didn't need to. The tension between them was palpable, the air charged with everything they hadn't said, with all the words they couldn't speak.

Lara didn't turn to face him. She couldn't. Not yet. The space between them felt like an ocean, and she didn't know how to bridge the gap.

"Elijah," she said finally, her voice trembling despite her best efforts to sound calm. "What's happening? What's going to happen to us? To me?"

There was a long pause. She could feel him standing behind her, could sense the hesitation in his movements, as though he were choosing his words carefully, afraid of saying too much, afraid of crossing some invisible line that would shatter what little remained between them.

"I don't want you to be a part of this," he said at last, his voice low, almost a whisper. "I never wanted this for you. I never wanted you to get caught in this... mess."

Lara's heart ached at the pain in his voice. She could hear the regret, the guilt—his sense of helplessness—but she couldn't ignore the fact that he had been keeping secrets from her. The same secrets that had now dragged her into a world of darkness she couldn't even begin to understand.

"You should have told me sooner," she said, her voice tight, betraying the raw emotion underneath. She felt the sting of his omission, the fear that perhaps she wasn't meant to be part of his world at all. "Why didn't you, Elijah?"

He stepped closer to her, and this time, she didn't pull away. His presence was a heavy weight behind her, a constant pull that she couldn't seem to resist. She could feel the warmth of his body just inches away, feel the tension radiating off of him.

"I thought I was protecting you," he said, his words like a confession, like a plea for understanding. "But I've been wrong about everything, Lara. I've been lying to myself. And now... now you're caught up in it, too."

Lara turned then, her eyes searching his face, looking for any sign of the man she thought she knew. But what she saw instead was a man at war with himself, a man broken by the very things he had tried to outrun.

"Tell me everything," she whispered. Her voice barely carried over the pounding of her heart. "All of it. I can't do this anymore—this… this guessing game. You owe me the truth."

He looked at her, his eyes dark with something unreadable, something deep and painful. For a moment, he said nothing. Then, as if the weight of it all had become too much to bear, he stepped back, dragging a hand through his hair in frustration.

"You don't understand. It's not just a curse," he said, his voice rising, breaking through the suffocating silence. "It's a chain, Lara. A chain that has been binding my family for generations. My father… he made a deal with something ancient, something dark. And the price was always the same. A life had to be taken."

Lara's breath caught in her throat. A life. Her life. She could feel the pieces falling into place, but the horror of the realization made her want to crumble to the floor. She didn't want to hear this. She didn't want to know the truth that was unfolding before her like a dark prophecy she had no way of stopping.

"What do you mean?" she asked, her voice trembling as she struggled to keep it steady. "Who had to die?"

"Elijah's father," he whispered, his voice raw, his words almost too painful to say aloud. "He bound our family to the curse.

Every generation, a Grayson has had to give up a life. It's always been this way. And now..." He looked away, his eyes filled with torment. "Now it's my turn. And it's... it's yours."

Lara's legs buckled beneath her, and she collapsed onto the couch, her breath coming in short, sharp gasps. The room spun around her, the walls seeming to close in. "No," she whispered. "No, Elijah, this isn't happening. This can't be real."

"I never wanted this," he said, his voice barely audible. "I never wanted you to be the one to pay the price. But the curse... it doesn't give us a choice. If I don't..." His voice faltered, breaking on the words. "If I don't follow through, if I don't make the sacrifice, the curse will claim everything. Everything we've built. Everything we love. It's not just about you, Lara. It's about all of us. It's about survival."

Lara shook her head, as if the motion could somehow stop the spiraling thoughts in her mind. Survival. A price that was too steep. A life for a life. Her life.

"Is that what you're willing to do?" she asked, her voice trembling, fear creeping into the corners of her words. "Is that how you see me? As a sacrifice?"

"No," Elijah said quickly, his voice full of anguish. He reached for her then, his hands trembling as they hovered just above hers, like he wasn't sure if he should touch her, if he deserved to. "No. You're not a sacrifice. You're... you're everything. But I don't have a choice. None of us do."

The Heart of Darkness

Lara looked at him, her heart pounding in her chest, her mind racing. She could feel the pull of him, the magnetic force that had always drawn her to him, but it felt different now. It felt heavier, darker. And in that moment, she realized that she had to make a choice. The same choice Elijah had made, whether he wanted to or not.

Her voice was a whisper when she spoke again, the words barely audible. "Then I'll make it. I'll make the sacrifice."

Elijah froze, his eyes wide with disbelief. "No," he whispered, his voice cracking. "I won't let you."

Lara stood, taking a step toward him, her heart thundering in her chest. "You don't get to make that decision for me, Elijah. I'll choose. I'll choose to stop this. Even if it means…" She faltered, the words too hard to say. Too final.

"Even if it means losing everything?" Elijah's voice was rough, like it had been dragged through fire. "Lara, you can't."

Lara reached for him, her fingers brushing his cheek, a last touch before the darkness closed in. "I can, Elijah. I will. Because in the end, this curse won't define me. And it won't define us."

The room seemed to grow colder, the shadows stretching toward them like fingers, pulling them both into the heart of the darkness. But in that moment, as their hands finally touched, as their hearts beat together in the quiet space between them, they both knew—there was no way out, only through. And the choice had already been made.

But the path ahead was uncertain. And nothing would ever be the same again.

Ten

The Final Veil

The air was thick with the scent of rain, the sharp, earthy aroma that lingered just after a storm. It had rained earlier that evening, leaving the streets slick and glistening under the fading lights of the city. But the night was still, heavy with expectation, as though the world held its breath, waiting for something—something that had been set in motion long before either Lara or Elijah had arrived.

Lara stood by the window, her gaze fixed on the distant skyline, where the dark silhouette of the city seemed to stretch endlessly. The light from the streetlamps below flickered in the distance, like the last remnants of hope in a world quickly slipping into shadows. Her mind was in turmoil, a whirlwind of emotions she couldn't name, but it all centered on one thing: the decision she had made. The choice that had been forced upon her.

She had chosen to sacrifice herself. To end the cycle of the curse. To save Elijah.

And yet, as the night pressed on, she found herself wondering whether she had made the right choice. Whether there was truly a way out, or if they were both being pulled deeper into a fate neither of them could control.

Behind her, she heard Elijah's footsteps approach, the soft, deliberate sound of his movements in the quiet room. His presence was like a weight on her chest, his every step a reminder of the bond they shared, of the love that had been forged in the midst of darkness. But that love—once a source of warmth, of safety—now felt like a tether, pulling her into an abyss she wasn't sure she could escape.

He stopped just behind her, close enough for her to feel the heat of his body, but far enough to maintain the space between them. The distance that had been growing ever since she had made her decision. Ever since the words had been spoken—sacrifice—and everything had changed.

"I'm sorry," Elijah's voice broke the silence, rough and full of pain. It was a confession, an apology, but it held something else, too—something darker. "I never should have let you be a part of this."

Lara's breath caught in her throat at the rawness in his tone. He had always carried the weight of the curse on his shoulders, but now it seemed that weight was threatening to crush him. She could feel it in the air, a suffocating pressure that seemed to close in around them both.

"You didn't make me part of this," she said softly, her voice trembling with emotion. She didn't turn to face him, not yet. She wasn't ready to meet his eyes, not when she knew what lay between them. Not when she knew that the decision she had made was one that would define everything. "I chose this. I chose you."

He was silent for a moment, and when he spoke again, his voice was laced with disbelief. "Why? Why would you do this for me, Lara?"

Lara finally turned to face him, her heart aching at the sight of the pain in his eyes. She reached out, her fingers trembling as they brushed against his arm, a touch so light, so tentative, as if she were afraid to break the fragile moment they shared.

"Because I love you," she said simply, the words falling from her lips as though they had always been there, waiting for the right moment to be spoken. "And I won't let this curse take you from me. I won't let it take us."

For a moment, Elijah seemed frozen, his eyes searching her face, as if he were trying to understand something that didn't make sense. His lips parted, but no words came out. Instead, he reached for her, pulling her into his arms in a way that felt like a lifeline, like he was desperate to hold onto her, to keep her close.

Lara closed her eyes as he enveloped her, the warmth of his

embrace comforting in a world that had grown so cold. She felt his heartbeat beneath her fingers, steady but filled with an underlying tension. He was afraid. Of losing her. Of losing everything.

"I can't lose you, Lara," he whispered against her hair, his voice breaking. "I can't."

She pulled back just slightly, enough to look into his eyes. "Then we fight," she said, her voice resolute. "We fight this. Together."

Elijah's eyes flickered, the faintest glimmer of hope flashing in the depths of their dark pools. But that hope was quickly extinguished as the sound of footsteps echoed outside the door. It was a slow, deliberate sound, a reminder that the world they were in was one of danger and uncertainty. And whatever lay beyond that door—whatever was coming—wasn't something they could ignore.

Elijah's body stiffened, his arms tightening around her for a moment before he gently pulled away. "Stay here," he whispered urgently. "Don't move."

Lara opened her mouth to protest, to argue, but he was already moving toward the door, his hand hovering over the doorknob as he turned back to her one last time. "Promise me, Lara. Stay here. No matter what."

She didn't know what to say. The promise he was asking of her felt like a thread she wasn't sure she could hold onto. She wanted to be with him. To stand by his side, no matter what came through that door. But something in his eyes, something in his expression, told her that he was preparing for something she couldn't even begin to understand.

"I promise," she said, her voice thick with emotion.

Elijah nodded, his expression unreadable, before he opened the door, stepping into the hallway without a backward glance. Lara's heart raced in her chest as the door clicked shut behind him, leaving her alone in the silence of the apartment. She felt like she was waiting on the edge of a precipice, knowing that once she crossed it, there would be no going back.

Minutes passed, or maybe hours—time seemed to blur, to stretch on in a way that made her feel untethered from reality. The air was thick, the tension suffocating, and Lara found herself pacing, her mind spinning, her heart thundering in her chest. She couldn't just sit here, not when she knew that whatever Elijah was facing out there could be the end of everything.

She stood in the middle of the room, her body tense, every muscle coiled in anticipation, when the door suddenly flew open. Elijah's silhouette filled the doorway, his form outlined by the dim light in the hall. But something was wrong. He was alone. And his face—his face was pale, drawn, like he had seen something that had drained the life from him.

"Lara," he breathed, his voice hoarse, filled with a rawness that sent a chill down her spine. "We're running out of time."

Lara's heart skipped a beat. "What happened?" she asked, her voice trembling as she stepped toward him. "What's going on?"

Elijah stepped into the room, closing the door behind him with a soft click, and for a moment, there was nothing but the sound of his ragged breathing, the weight of the world in the air between them.

"They're coming," he said, his voice filled with a terrible certainty. "The ones who control the curse. The ones who are waiting for me to fulfill it."

Lara's stomach dropped, the cold fear wrapping around her heart like a vice. She could feel the darkness closing in, the suffocating presence of something she didn't fully understand but knew she was about to face.

"And they want you, Lara," Elijah said, his voice breaking. "They won't stop until they have you."

In that moment, the walls of the apartment felt like they were closing in, the weight of everything pressing down on them both. The final veil had been lifted, and what lay beyond it was a truth neither of them could escape.

The curse was coming for them. And there was nothing left to do but face it—together.

Lara took a deep breath, her resolve hardening. She stepped closer to Elijah, her hand finding his in the darkness. She could feel his fingers trembling, but she squeezed his hand tightly, grounding them both in this moment, in this fight.

"We'll face it," she whispered, her voice steady despite the fear clawing at her insides. "Together."

And with that, they stepped into the unknown, side by side.

Eleven

Embraced by Light

The cold wind howled through the cracks of the apartment, a wild, mournful sound that seemed to echo the turmoil inside Lara's chest. Once familiar and safe, the walls now felt like they were closing in on her, suffocating her with the weight of everything that had happened. Elijah stood by the window, his back to her, his posture rigid and tense. His figure was framed by the city lights that glowed faintly beyond the glass, casting his shadow like a dark silhouette against the cold night.

Lara stood still, her fingers nervously twisting the hem of her shirt, watching him silently. She could feel the growing distance between them, which wasn't just physical. It was in the air, thick and heavy, like the first tremor of a storm about to break. And she didn't know how to bridge it.

The curse, the sacrifice, the darkness that had settled into their lives, pulling them both deeper into its depths—all of it swirled in her mind, a maelstrom of fear and uncertainty. And yet, through it all, one thing had remained constant—their connection—the undeniable pull between them. It had brought them together, and now, it seemed to be the one thing holding them from being swallowed entirely by the chaos.

"Elijah?" Her voice broke the silence, barely above a whisper, but it was enough to make him flinch.

He didn't turn to her immediately, and for a long moment, she wondered if he even heard her. But then, slowly, his shoulders relaxed, and he faced her, his expression unreadable. She could see the weight of the battle raging inside him—the battle between what he had to do and what he wanted to do. It was a war he'd been fighting for far too long, and now, she was caught in the crossfire.

"You shouldn't be here," he said quietly, his voice low, heavy with regret. "This is not your fight. I never wanted you to be part of it."

Lara's heart ached at the words, at the finality in his tone. She knew he was trying to protect her—he always had been—but she wasn't the same woman she had been when they first met. The world they were now living in, the world they had been pulled into, was no longer one where she could stand on the sidelines. She had already made her choice.

"I'm already in it, Elijah," she said, her voice firm, though the tremor of fear she felt inside threatened to crack her composure. "I'm already with you. Whatever this curse is, whatever it demands from us, we face it together. We always face it together."

His eyes flickered, the briefest moment of something—desperation, maybe?—flashing behind the dark pools. He stepped closer to her, but still, there was a barrier between them, an invisible wall that neither of them seemed able to breach. The space between them pulsed with the weight of unspoken words, of emotions that had been buried so deep neither of them knew how to dig them back up.

Lara took a step forward, closing the gap between them, her heart racing with every inch. "Don't push me away," she said softly, her voice steady but filled with an intensity that was impossible to ignore. "Not now. Not when we're this close."

Elijah's gaze dropped to the floor, his hands clenched at his sides as if he were fighting with every part of himself to hold onto something—anything—that would keep him from breaking. The silence between them stretched longer, unbearable in its weight. And then, finally, he looked up, his eyes filled with pain and something darker, something like a deep-seated guilt that threatened to consume him.

"I'm not pushing you away," he whispered, his voice hoarse. "I'm trying to keep you safe. But there's no escaping this. There's no way out. You don't understand. This curse—it's alive. It's a living thing, and it's been hunting my family for generations."

Lara's heart sank, her breath hitching as the words echoed in her mind. She had known it was bad. She had known it was dangerous. But to hear him say it like that—to hear him speak of it like it was some kind of living entity, something with its own mind, its own will—it made everything feel so much worse.

"It's not just about me," Elijah continued, his voice growing more urgent, more desperate. "I've spent my entire life running from this, trying to find a way to end it. But now... now it's come for you, Lara. And I don't know if I can protect you. I don't know if I can protect either of us anymore."

Lara reached for him, her fingers grazing his arm, the touch gentle but filled with the weight of everything they had shared. "You don't have to protect me, Elijah," she said, her voice barely a whisper. "We're in this together. And I'm not leaving. Not now. Not when you need me the most."

For a moment, the world seemed to stop. Time hung suspended between them, the seconds stretching into eternity as they stood there, caught in the storm that had been brewing for so long. Elijah's eyes softened, the hardness in them giving way to something more vulnerable, more human.

And then, without warning, he closed the distance between them, his arms wrapping around her in a sudden, desperate embrace. Lara gasped, the force of it catching her off guard, but she didn't pull away. She pressed herself closer to him, her hands fisting in the fabric of his shirt, as though trying to hold on to him, to keep him from slipping through her fingers.

"I don't want to lose you," Elijah murmured against her hair, his voice breaking. "I don't want to lose anyone I love."

Lara's heart clenched at the words, at the raw emotion in them. She pulled back just enough to look at him, her fingers brushing his cheek, tracing the lines of pain that marred his once-perfect face.

"You won't lose me," she said softly, her voice steady despite the fear that still curled in her chest. "I'm here, Elijah. I'm not going anywhere."

But as the words left her mouth, she felt it—felt the change in the air. The room seemed to shift, the temperature dropping sharply, the weight of something heavy pressing down on them both. It was as if the very walls were closing in, the silence becoming too much to bear. Her heart raced in her chest, her breath coming faster as a chill swept through the room, cutting through the warmth of their embrace.

And then she heard it.

A sound, faint at first, but growing louder with every passing second. The scraping of metal, the echo of something far too close. Her breath caught in her throat as the realization hit her: they weren't alone. The curse—the force that had been chasing Elijah's family for generations—was no longer waiting. It had come.

Elijah pulled back, his eyes wide with recognition, his face drained of color. "They're here," he said, his voice barely above a whisper. "They're coming for us."

Lara's heart pounded in her chest, her limbs frozen in place. The fear she had been trying to suppress rose up in a tidal wave, flooding her senses, making it hard to breathe, to think. She knew what it meant. She knew what was happening.

And then, the door crashed open.

A figure stood in the doorway, cloaked in shadows, the outline of a person almost indistinguishable from the darkness itself. The air grew colder still, the very presence of the figure a tangible force that seemed to crush the air around them.

Elijah stepped in front of Lara, instinctively shielding her, but Lara wasn't afraid. Not anymore. Not with him beside her.

"I've been waiting for this moment," the figure said, its voice low, guttural, as if it had been carved from the depths of some dark abyss. "You thought you could outrun the curse. But it was always meant to end this way."

Lara could feel the pulse of the curse now, feel it thrumming in the air like a living, breathing entity. She reached for Elijah's hand, squeezing it tightly, and though fear still gripped her heart, she knew one thing with absolute certainty:

They would face this together. And whatever came through that door, they would fight it—together.

There was no turning back.

Twelve

Embraced by the Shadows

The room felt like it was shrinking. The air had thickened with the weight of the figure standing in the doorway, its presence a dark, oppressive force that pushed against Lara's chest, making it hard to breathe. Her pulse hammered in her ears, but she didn't take her eyes off the figure before them. It was as if the darkness itself had materialized, its edges blurred, its form shifting in the dim light. She could feel the air grow colder with every passing second, the temperature dropping sharply, the chill seeping into her skin, into her bones.

Elijah stepped in front of her, his body tense, his stance protective, but Lara could sense his uncertainty. This wasn't just any enemy. This was something older, something deeper—something they could neither outrun nor escape.

Embraced by the Shadows

"Who are you?" Elijah's voice was sharp, but it trembled slightly, betraying the fear he had been trying to hide. His hand curled into a fist at his side, ready to strike, but even he seemed unsure of what exactly to do. He was caught between wanting to protect her and the reality that they were standing at the edge of something he couldn't control.

The figure in the doorway did not answer immediately. Instead, it stepped forward, its movements slow and deliberate, as though savoring the moment. It was cloaked in shadows, its features indistinct, but there was something undeniably powerful about its presence—something ancient and unforgiving.

"You've been running for so long," the figure's voice crooned, low and unnerving, like the rasp of dry leaves in the wind. "But there is no running from what you've become. The curse is in your blood, Elijah. It always has been. And now it has come for her."

Lara's heart dropped at the words, a chill racing down her spine. Her. She didn't have to ask who the figure meant. The curse, the curse that had bound Elijah's family for generations, was coming for her. She had known that the moment she'd made her choice. But hearing it, hearing it spoken aloud, made it real. And terrifying.

"Don't touch her," Elijah growled, stepping forward, his chest heaving with a mixture of fear and determination. His gaze was locked on the figure, his body radiating tension as if he were ready to lunge, to fight. But Lara knew it wasn't that simple. There was power here—power beyond anything either of them had ever faced.

The figure didn't seem threatened. Instead, it tilted its head, the movement unnervingly human in its fluidity. "You think you can protect her?" it murmured. "You think that love will save her? It never saves anyone. Love is only a weakness, Elijah. A weakness you can't afford when you've made a deal with darkness."

Lara's breath quickened as she stepped closer to Elijah, the sudden urge to stand by him, to be his strength, almost overwhelming. She wasn't going to be afraid. Not anymore. She had chosen this. Chosen him. And she would not back down.

The figure took another step closer, its presence pulling at the very air around them. Lara could feel it now, deep in her chest—a weight, a pressure, like something was closing in, tightening its grip on her, on both of them.

"You don't understand," Elijah said through clenched teeth, his voice low and strained, but there was a fierce fire in it. "I don't care about the curse. I don't care about your power. I care about her. And I will fight for her."

The figure chuckled softly, the sound like the scrape of nails on glass. It was mocking, as if it knew something Elijah didn't. "You think you can escape your bloodline? Escape your fate?" The voice was thick with venom. "You are nothing but the tool of an ancient force, Elijah. And now… it's time to pay the price. All of it. Including her."

Lara's heart skipped in her chest, a terrible, cold realization sinking in. The figure was right. The curse—the force that had haunted Elijah's family for generations—was tied to her now. And there was no escaping it. Not for her, not for Elijah. The cycle of death and rebirth, the price that had to be paid with every generation, had come for her. And no matter how much she fought, how much she loved Elijah, there was no way out.

But she wouldn't give up. Not without a fight.

"Don't you dare touch her," Elijah hissed, his voice sharp, commanding. The power in his words was like a crack in the air. She could feel it. The moment the words left his lips, the temperature in the room dropped even lower, the shadows in the corners of the room seeming to deepen, thicken, like they were coming to life.

The figure's smile widened, a sickeningly slow curve of its lips, as if it were enjoying the tension, the fear. "I'm not here to touch her, Elijah," it said, its voice soft but heavy with finality. "I'm here to end this. To end what you started."

Lara stepped forward then, her hand finding Elijah's, her fingers trembling but firm. "You'll have to go through me first," she said, her voice clear and steady despite the storm raging inside her. She could feel her heart pounding in her chest, the echo of it in her ears, but there was no time for fear. Not now. Not when they had come this far.

The figure turned its gaze to her, and for a moment, it was as if time itself slowed. The darkness in the room seemed to grow even darker, like the very walls were breathing, closing in. The figure's eyes glowed faintly, the faintest flicker of something—something ancient, something beyond the mortal realm—flickering in the abyss of its gaze.

"You think you're strong enough to stand against this, Lara?" The figure's voice was soft now, almost a whisper, but it held a deadly edge. "You're just a pawn in this game. A piece in a much larger picture. You can't change what's already been set into motion."

Lara's grip on Elijah's hand tightened. She wasn't afraid. Not anymore. "I don't care what you say. I'm not going anywhere. And neither is Elijah."

For a moment, the figure said nothing. It only watched them, its presence like a shadow pressing against their skin, suffocating, but there was something else in its gaze now. A flicker of uncertainty. And in that moment, Lara understood.

The figure didn't know what she was capable of. It didn't understand the power of love, of choice. It thought it could control them, manipulate them into submitting to the curse, but it had underestimated them both.

With a sudden movement, the figure stepped back, its eyes narrowing, its form flickering like smoke. For a moment, it almost seemed to dissolve into the shadows, but then, its voice filled the room, more menacing than ever.

"This isn't over, Lara. You may have delayed it, but the curse will claim what it's owed. It always does."

The figure vanished, as if it had never been there at all, leaving nothing but the cold, oppressive silence behind.

Lara stood frozen, her breath shallow, her body trembling from the adrenaline that still coursed through her veins. But she didn't look at Elijah. She couldn't.

Instead, she felt his hand on her shoulder, turning her toward him. His face was pale, but there was a fire in his eyes—a fire that matched her own. He didn't say anything at first, but she could feel his heart racing, just as hers was. The terror that had gripped them both moments ago was still there, still lingering in the air between them.

And yet, despite it all, despite the terror of the curse and the darkness that had crept into their lives, she could still feel it—the bond between them, the unbreakable tie forged in the fire of their love. They had made it this far. And together, they would face whatever came next.

Elijah pulled her into his arms, his embrace strong and steady, grounding her in the chaos. She closed her eyes, pressing her face against his chest, feeling the steady beat of his heart beneath her ear. The world outside was dark and uncertain, but in his arms, she found something she hadn't realized she needed—hope. Hope that no matter what, they would fight this. Together.

"We'll face it," Elijah whispered into her hair, his voice filled with a fierce determination. "We'll face it together, Lara."

And in that moment, as they stood there, wrapped in each other's arms, Lara knew with an undeniable certainty that they would. They had to. Because no matter how dark the world became, they were stronger than the shadows. They were stronger than the curse.

And they would fight until the very end.

www.ingramcontent.com/pod-product-compliance
Lightning Source LLC
LaVergne TN
LVHW020430080526
838202LV00055B/5114